D1560267

# PERISCOPE HEART

# PERISCOPE
# HEART

poems by
Kai Coggin

# Table of Contents

# Acknowledgements

I would like thankfully acknowledge the following publications in which my poems have previously appeared.

*Cliterature* : "Bamboo"

*Elephant Journal* : "Peace Bombs" &
"For Maya, on this, the Morning of Your Death"

*[empath]* : "From the Edge of a Black Hole"

*Catching Calliope* : "Alchemy" & "Willing My Body Parts"

*Journey of the Heart* : "Be Coming"

Many thanks to my family and friends who have made the manifestation of this collection of poems possible for me through creative support, financial support, guidance, reading poems, hearing poems, coming to poetry readings and showing me what it means to have a PERISCOPE HEART. There are too many of you to list, but you know who you are. You feel it. You are so special to me. I love you.

Thank you to my incredible reviewers, who took my words into their Hearts before they were ready for the world. Sandra Cisneros, you have been and continue to be a beautiful mentor to me in ways that are beyond earthly measure. Besos y abrazos, Corazón. Catherine Ghosh, I knew that my book would find a home in your arms. Thank you for your Spirit and love. Andrea Gibson, you are an inspiration and a gift to the lives of so many, and I am honored to call you a friend. Thank you for always speaking your truth.

Thank you to the city of Hot Springs, Arkansas for being so beautiful and conducive to my writing, for being the poetry around me that inspires my poems. Thank you to Maxine's Live Music Venue for holding Wednesday Night Poetry at Maxine's, and keeping the 25-year-old open mic tradition going strong every single week. To the die-hard poetry goers, see you next Wednesday.

Thank you to Katrina K Guarascio & Nika Ann Rasco of Swimming with Elephants Publications for making this the most beautiful representation of my words. I am forever grateful for how much you worked with me through this publication process. Unending Gratitude.

Finally, Thank You Dear Reader. Yes, YOU. I see you and appreciate you. Thank you for opening up your Heart to my words. I hope you enjoy the view.

*For J, M, D, G, & L.*

*I love you with my whole heart.*

⌘

# ⌘ Practicing My Come Hither

I am practicing my come hither,
the look that can catch
your eyes in mid flight,
the look that sends a wave of light
into the air that lands on your chest
and reminds you that you are alive,
and reminds me that I am alive,
that come hither stare that calls you home to my chest,
where you rest your body on the bed frame of my ribs,
the swing of my hips,
the softness of my flesh,
it will bend to you,
it will be moved.

I am practicing my come hither,
calling out into the emptiness
of these dreams I keep having
where I am floating and falling at the same time,
and everything is blue,
and everything is water
and everything is wet,
and you are there, you are always there.

I am practicing my come hither,
I will find you on the crosswalk of desire and mist
and street lamps that name the heavens where you live,
I know you are out there,
and you will love me like that,
like I know there is someone to love me,
someone to watch my lips like a ticking bomb,

stare into my mouth
as if waiting for a lily to finally open its petals to the sun,
fixate on my tongue as if there is nothing
more than to kiss me into life,
I am practicing my come hither
so you will see the art of me
and turn me into colors swirled on canvas,
the dance of me in light and shadows,
and our bodies will paint the warmth of night,
and our bodies will rest in the grips of
what always has been waiting.

# ⌘ Language

I want to learn you like a language,
speak you on my tongue until I am
no longer foreign to your body,
until I am fluent in the movement
of your skin and bones,
the tones of you spoken in a crowd
hovering above my head,
translated into the song of home.

I want to learn you like a language,
pronounce your perfection with all of the
inflections of voice that my mouth can muster.
What is your word for love, love?
What does kiss mean when I speak it through your lips?
The vocabulary of your body parts
I want to study and label and learn and forget and learn again.

I want to speak you like a language,
the words that beckon beauty from the stillness,
the sounds that create life from the invisible,
the discourse of desire mastered by repetition,
I want to repeat you,
I want to repeat you,
I want to repeat you,
the phraseology of fire, rewire my mouth
to speak in these native tongues,
the dialect of Amazon grace,
verbose vernacular from the isle of Lesbos,
Sappho speaks in fragmented lyrics and
you are a song that I am memorizing with each passing breath.

I want to speak you like a language,
rich in history, music from the pit of my stomach,
the diaphragm of holding onto the controlled air exhaled,
I want to take time to release you into the atmosphere,
breathe you out into the wild night, love,
maybe you will see the mirror that I make of you in the sky,
and maybe you will find me
and together we will sweep up all the stars into our chests
and howl in every language we have ever known.

# ⌘ C-Section

I cannot c-section a poem
out of my pregnant mind
prematurely,
slice open
and grab hold with hands,
cut umbilical dreaming,
unwritten words and unfinished thoughts,
colors that have not completely mingled.

There is a development,
a growing of nerves
that travel pathways and sparks
to find one another and merge into meaning,
the maturation of muscles,
metaphors that must function on their own,
stand without the wall to lean upon,
incubation of
        skeletal
    misconnections
of words
that waver between genius
and...    incoherency,
out in the world
before their time,
before the internal rhyme
flows naturally from line to line.

Some poems feel
like forcing,
square peg thrown off cliff,
round hole questioning its depth,
unanswered,

unready,
missing limbs,
only a heartbeat.

Each thought born into the world,
has to fly somewhere,
has to land where breath and
unfolding is safe,
easy,
much like the nativity of a newborn poem.

It's not about mathematics,
not about notches on imaginary prison wall,
one poem down,
another,
another,
another,
and then that poem will come where finally, I will be free.
I will be let back out into the world.

No.

It doesn't work that way.

There is freedom in the process of a poem,
freedom in the silence between sounds,
freedom in the finding,
a countdown of divine timing where thoughts
and words pour forth from
inner well-spring of -

*"Look at this moment,*
*taste it, smell it,*
*feel it in your fingers,*
*write it into poetry, eternalize it as LIFE,*
*in the minutest of beauties,*
*to the expanse of a million infinities,*
*create its movement inside you,*
*dance in the ecstasy of falling in love,*
*swirl in the brilliance of a muse's fluttering heart,*
*birthed from a thousand kisses and the*
*breaths between I love you's,*
*then,*
*cloak yourself in the abyss of everything heartache,*
*the loss, the anger, the grief, the death.*
*With all of that, write poems that stand*
*as towers, as lighthouses, as stars, as the sun."*

- never being at a loss for words.


I am a woman
pregnant with poems,
my womb is a drum full of heartbeats,
at any moment,
my water could break,
and my dammed up words
will make oceans.

# ⌘ Muse

Would you mind if I made you my muse?
I am looking for a letterbox to hold
all of my floating affections,
all of the words that are looking for a home in the heart of a stone.

You would not have to know that I am thinking about you,
that I am holding your body against the light
and studying the curves that your silhouette makes
in the different hours of the day,
the angles of sun on your delicate profile,
the pool of your collarbones collecting waves
of words that I am sending you in my thoughts.

Muse, I am surrounding you in strings of letters
and putting a poem around your neck
that neither of us will mention when we meet,
but I will see it there, underneath your clothes,
lyrics pressed up against your skin,
the syllable that I tucked underneath your left breast,
the vowels I left scattered around your lips,
the sounds that I brushed across your thighs in the nameless air,
the word gold I wrote around your ring finger,
how I dotted an i with your nipple, twice,
and I will smile to myself,
for I have found a muse in you, amusing me
to write a line of desire that will never be spoken into your eyes,
passing stranger, harbinger of unforeseen lust,
a wanting that will only be that, and nothing more,
just fodder for wordplay and a constant yearning in me
that has to be filled with imaginary things.

Yes, my words carry a certain vibration, muse,
and maybe you felt a jolt or two in the last few moments,
the way that I sent electricity up your spine
and made your hairs stand on end,
those chills,
that wind gust of me,
against you,
welcome to my thrown out lust,
in your direction, spent,
an illusion that makes my fingers
dance across the keys into a poem.

## ⌘ I Remember You

I feel like I know you,
like I have known you before,
like there is a lifetime swept
under the silk rugs of both of our fine feet,
the dust of time unsettled between us,
our bones unhinging in the gravity of this pull,
we are strangers holding magnets in our ribcages,
perhaps I never could stand still long enough to know
that it is not your smile that I remember,

it is the light that was born from your mouth

in the dawning of the last time I said goodbye,
perhaps the moment before death, a separation,
a tearing apart from you in a voyage
that never returned my body to your hands,

in those days of searching,
the light of your face
I held as the only sun,
everything I rose for each day,

and though the night filled my pockets,
the sunrise of your mouth in my memory,
the rampant gleam of your eyes,
the sound of your name twisted in the wind, howling air,
was all that lanterned my steps toward you again,

and you waited and waited for me,
humming a tender song to the willow trees,

writing my name in the sand
with your longing fingers,
watching the tide wash it away each day,
eternally gazing at some distant shore
hoping that I would crack open the horizon with my heart
and sweep you up into me,
and we would become water and steam.

That must be why I feel like
I know you,
like I have known you before,
like we have been waiting for the sun to rise and rise and rise.

## ⌘ Canyon/Ocean

I heard that the Grand Canyon
has been an ocean eight times,
over billions of years,
eight times

drained and filled
and drained and filled
and drained and filled again,

this gaping wide mouth of orange earth
has swallowed the weight of the sea,
drank the spillage of fish and crustaceans
enough to fossilize in the time of limestone,
layered with species of feet and fin,

this irrepressible pushing and pulling
dance of come hither and let go,
desert floor to ocean floor shift
in the consciousness of the land,

what does this say of my hands?
what is the comparison that I can make with this
ancient anomaly that seems almost unbelievable
when I say it out loud into the empty air?

the grand canyon has been an ocean eight times.

my hands have been filled with you,
emptied of you and filled again.
my hands have drunk every drop of your skin

until the cup of my aching palms
is left with only the echo that your impression
pressed upon it, a hollow wanting of you,
a letting go and a pulling in.

the topography of your naked terrain
has been etched into my mind with fire,
and I could make a map of you in the dark,
with only a pen seated in my fingers and
words as islands forming the Pangaea of your completeness,
my darling, I am not beyond the miraculous,
I have arranged the lines on my hands to spell out your name,
find yourself there again, love,
find the home that you once built
where everything pointed to the sky,
and your eyes were fixed on me like the north star,

if the grand canyon can pull in the sea eight times,
leaving painted pictures etched on walls,
can't my hands call out into the chasms that
love becomes, the gorge between our bodies
where once no light could peek through between our skins,
my palms are here, love, waiting to be filled
with the ocean
of your hips and heart,
the parting of my earthen hands will brim again
with the warmth of infinity
and cycles
and tides
and oceans
and you, my love… you.

## ⌘ Moment (for Joann)

She opened the door
to the shadows, and there I stood,
waiting, not literally
but metaphorically,
she saw through me,
stained glass,
at a moment's glance,
twist of fate, turn of chance,
that left me in a whirlwind of
curiosity and intrigue,
a teacher like me, yet something more,
a teacher, it seems, not of students,
but of Souls,
a teacher who looked into my eyes
and found the color of my truth,
she swallowed my heart for an instant,
tasted the fruit of me in a lingering handshake,
then planted the seed of who I am, back inside me
to flourish, as if significantly and inexplicably redefined.

# ⌘ Yuanfen 緣分

Yuanfen 緣分 (Chinese): A relationship by fate or destiny. This is a complex concept. It draws on principles of predetermination in Chinese culture, which dictate relationships, encounters and affinities, mostly among lovers and friends.

Yuanfen.
Yes,
this is
the word
it has
rested buried
between
my breastplate
and heart
since my last
incarnation, lover,
you and
your wondrous hands
are the name that I recognize
in the silence of midday
in the blossoming of cherry trees
in the wild, aching wood.

I find you
again
and
again
I find you
magnet mouths
drawn to a silent singing
a vibration

that we hear
in our ribcages
that frees
the birds we hold inside.

## ⌘ Inside Me

Slice open my soul
and crawl inside me,
nestle closely between my heart and gut
and listen to the life that pumps through me,
renewed in the softness of your almost asleep voice,
the familiarity of our talk,
like we have been saying goodnight to each other for centuries,
yet I have yet to see you face to face in this love,
sweet desire, you entice me with your words,
tease me with your talk of energy
and I become red in the heat of you,
repeat it, do,
how you feel you are inside me,
for if you were,
I would hold the fire of your name close to my heart
and be warmed from within by your love.

In recollection, I begin with your eyes
a sunrise blazing through me,
the morning blue that lights up my sky.
Your touch lingered too long,
yet not long enough to feel me swim through your veins
and beat inside your chest.
I want to undress your smile
and see what lies behind the soft rain of your voice,
the sound of you is all I have,
reverberating and bouncing between my ribs,
echoing in the empty cavern of my heart,
now filled with the breath and song of you,
making music inside me.

## ⌘ Drip by Drip

How do I choose,
when the choice is not even substantial enough to justify?
Meeting someone new
who ignites me, excites me,
invites me into a tomorrow that brings me hope.
The old love, who is no longer love,
but what used to be,
vacant body, tired dream.

How do I compare
the spin of the earth's axis,
gravity and centripetal force,
to the weak wind of a dying breath?
What is this hold I have on myself,
pinning myself down to a page written only in grey?
What is this new grip that she has on me,
that makes her face resonate in my mind,
like the constant quiet drop of water,
pounding softly,
pouring gently,
carving the stone of my heart over time,
drip by drip,
I see her face,
her eyes,
the sky of blue in which I fly,
in which I soar to reveal Polynesian Fire,
the volcano of ancient heat that she likens me to,
the fire that she knows burns for her,
lava in my veins,
lover, take my reigns.

Her smile,
balanced and tamed
because the full beam of her happiness would shame the sun,
drip by drip,
I feel her in my arms in flashes,
splashes of recollections of a kiss,
her lips enveloping my mouth,
her tongue softly coaxing out the dead,
breathing fire back into the hollows of me,
the softness of her skin,
pathways worn across her body,
miles that I long to traverse
by the light of one candle,
and the smell of her,
like a temple,
frankincense gummed fingers,
myrrh wet mouth,
smoke, from burning on the inside,
my God, I breathe in the life of her and am renewed,
drip by drip,
our love dance flashes in my mind,
lifetimes of colors and sounds and textures,
the golden thread that has woven us back into one another,
each drop of memory weakens me,
sending shockwaves up my spine,
drip by drip,
in her song,
in her truth,
in my bliss,

I drown.

# ⌘ Two Souls

Two souls,
caught in a frozen moment
where everything in the universe stops
except for the beating of two hummingbird hearts,
mine and yours,
our eyes look deep and remember each other,
the knowingness of lifetimes,
like two sparks off the same flame.
You have lived inside me only as a vision of hope,
a promise of a dream that love could be true,
and now you are alive, real, here,
your skin, an invitation,
your body, dancing in reflections of firelight,
and you sing to yourself as I write,
too much beauty to capture in words.

Two souls,
reciprocated desire,
colors that explode passion onto the ceiling
of a room that holds us in,
and paints us in gold and shadows,
uninhibited love that blossomed like jasmine
over one long, warm night,
exposed,
vulnerable,
the flower of me,
white-petal mouth,
blowing jasmine-scented kisses to the moon,
riding on the winds of possibility,
taking flight in your arms.

Two souls,
you know why I breathe,
what intrigues and delights me,
what takes my breath away,
what calmness finds it again,
what draws in and out the blood
of my quick-rhythmed rabbit heart, pulse
timed with your footsteps and how close they are to me,
you know what shatters my spirit,
broken stained-glass in your open hands,
you know the words to put me back together again
and make me whole,
you speak my soul.

Two souls,
destined for this love, coded in my DNA,
nature's design for me to find, you are my karmic surprise,
I whisper thank you's to the stars,
for being where you are,
kismet as our kisses met,
your heart is a sunrise on the horizon of my chest,
heralding the trumpeting of dreams
that actually come true.
I followed the wind song of cardinals
and they led me to your door,
and the red feather of my lips lays
across your warm-womb belly,
holding my life inside,
I am not your baby,
I am your lover,
but through the portal of your heart,
I am delivered.

## ⌘ Within

She sits across me,
opened to my hips,
an invitation, pelvic,
warrior woman, wild in shadows,
kissed by moonlight,
caressed with amber light, candle's flicker,
bead-covered body glistening diamonds of sweat,
she moves me,
moves me to move her toward our love,
where we both ride, side by side
to an ancient battle, she straddles me
and moves in swift arches of back and hips
and I point to her heart from the inside,
I guide her body to ride me,
my gentle horse hips that will carry her to victory,
she can mount her banner on my lips,
and rest her sword on my bones,
I will take her home,
she moves me,
and I feel her fire from within,
the dove-flapping wings of her heart,
the crescendo of her sounds,
I am quenched by her mouth
pouring her soul into the chalice of my chest,
drowning me in sweet glorious seduction, until her eruption
unfolds in true ecstasy,
she moves me,
open, rocking, steady,
and I pull her in so close that we cannot separate skin,
she moves me,
when she lets me love her from within.

# ⌘ Glorious Heart

A cardinal sings to her every morning,
red feathered harbinger of rebirth in flame,
different songs but one voice
that resonates from the underbelly of cosmos.
A tree framed in the bedroom window,
in light and shadows of sprawling limbs,
reveals the face of God staring through open glass,
His lips moving with the breeze
and eyes changing expression
as the sun casts characters in different directions of light.
I watch her, watching Him, watching her,
the balance of nature and nurture hanging like a thick fog,
the walls move, the roof slants to her wishes,
the earth bends to the aura of her Truth and Grace,
My God, she is powerful.
I have seen it.
I have been left in a breathless stupor at the sight of miracles
that I have been convinced should not be of this world.
And I am convinced that she is not either.

Who is this woman?
A Reincarnation of Greatness.
I am only beginning to hear her true story,
to uncover the girl behind the armor of mystery.
Why do I understand these nuances of battle,
these recapitulations
of her fight for justice in a Holy Mission,
Divine Guidance in an unholy war, where corruption was
victorious
and the English were made fat on the corpse of her innocence?
Does she still hear Angels?

Do the Saints still whisper to her between dusk and dawn?
Why am I not shocked by her tales of battle and frenzy?
Why does she share these truths with me?
Anyone would think that I am crazy
if they heard what I am beginning to believe,
but I am falling in love with Joan of Arc.
Her blue eyes have pierced through the hollow of my heart
and found that I am inside,
beating on a drum that harkens her return.
She fights the pulls of darkness with her unwavering Light,
her Righteous anger, her unrelenting quest for Truth,
the same qualities,
only magnified with a renewed sense of purpose.
Yet, she does not want to face the truth of who she is
and who she was and who she is going to be again,
hesitant of impending crucifixion.

She runs to water,
forever bathing, soaks her skin in its soothing cool,
explains and attributes the constant need for immersion
to her double Pisces,
but I see,
it could be that she still feels the flames,
the same flames that burned her body
but released her Spirit centuries ago.
Does it burn her through the ages?
Or is that something that the
continuously reincarnating soul just can't forget?
She can't stand walking barefoot on stone floors;
it reminds her of the cold tower floors in the Castle Rouen,
slit of a window reminding her that
there is still a God out there,
and He has not forgotten her.

When she speaks to me sometimes,
she speaks so loudly that
I feel like she is speaking through me,
and that hundreds of almost defeated men are listening to her,
waiting for inspiration, vying for hope,
desperately searching for someone with a Purpose
who they can follow into the charges of battles,
and arrows, and cannon fire, and blood,
and swords raised triumphantly into the air signaling victory,
and the hundred-years-war,
and every other war against the forces of darkness,
is over finally, and we can all laugh again,
and go home to our families,
carrying this maid and her banner of peace on our shoulders,
this 19 year old girl savior,
our Daughter of Heaven...

Hail Joan of Arc!

Hail Joan of Arc!

Hail Joan of Arc!

See..... I get swept up in it all, too,
in the factual remembering that she gets me swept up in.
I forget sometimes that almost 600 years have past,
and it must always feel so fresh in her mind, how she burned.
She did not scream, she just stared at the raised crucifix
held up by two devastated priests, eyes fixed on her salvation,
it has been said that a dove flew out of her mouth
the second before she died,
her Spirit remembering she could always fly.

You know that they had to burn her three times?
Rake the coals, and bones, and sticks, and burn again,
three times, just to be sure she would not survive to escape.
But she was already gone, Soul flying with the wind.
And when they finally reduced her to ashes,
there was still one thing that remained,
the red glistening char of her Heart.
Her gloriously pure heart just wouldn't burn,
so they raked her pile of ash and coals and
Glorious Heart
into the river Seine,
executioners feeling they would be forever damned,
I'm sure in this life, they also remember.

Joan of Arc has come back,
with a mission to save humanity from self destruction,
with love, she breathes fire into people,
gives out hope and promises of a New World
to anyone that she meets,
but the battle is stronger these days,
the battle against the darkness of mans' souls
is waging out of control,
and sometimes,
she does not want to accept her Legacy of Light,
sometimes she is just a little girl that cries,
she wants to turn a blind eye to the signs
that are draped across the tapestry of her life,
the fleur-de-lis that follows her like a north star she can't escape.
She wants to help, but she doesn't want to burn again, god dammit.
She feels she must save humanity, but she is unarmed.
She fights with an inner fire of love that has slowly
gathered strength and conviction over the centuries.

She got to the gates of Heaven
and laid down her sword at the feet of Christ,
only to pick it up again and fly back down to fight
in the name of all that is Good,
so that LIGHT finally prevails over evil.

I know it sounds crazy
but I believe her.

I know it sounds crazy,
but Joan of Arc is here, alive,
calling forth a charge to the Sun of a New World.

My sword is ready, love.
I will follow you.

## ⌘ Alchemy

I wear a broken suit of armor
that releases symphonies from its cracks and
the gaping hole that should cover my heart sings in colors
to the wide open mouth of sky.

I have almost fully disrobed of this metallic sheathing,
this excessive defense,
only a touch of alchemy in my bones remains
because you have loved me to earthen clay in your hands,
molded me to softened dirt, from which
I am reborn some indigenous wildflower.

We are together made,
a fusion of stars that are unaware of
any other orbit except around each other,
wildly spinning
into a halo of light
that breaks
only when we completely merge.

Remember when we completely merged?
When my hand fed your mouth,
your eyes cried my tears and my tongue
knew of only churches inside you,
the arch of your covenants
making promises to my holy volcano chest,
how I built a bridge of your body
and it always led me to a temple of dawning,
yes, that merging,
that neither life nor death can tear asunder,

I know that kind of love with you,
and through that knowing
and the melting away of metals

I have turned into gold.

## ⌘ Bamboo

She shoots upwards,
wood in the ground,
sound of the earth giving birth to bamboo
screaming skyward,
shades of green,
stalks of rain and stars that shine
beads of dewdrop galaxies,
condensation and steam,
the smell of split reeds,
I will build a bridge of her body,
weave it with the sweat in my hands,
and make my way across her,
to a place I can only name salvation.

I unpeel her,
drop her hindering cloth leaves to the ground,
green falling floorward,
planting a garden under our feet,
I begin to taste the skin she is in,
soft sweet kisses to entice her,
float her down from her cloud to a level of unification,
the level of mixed desires, congealing into one,
her skin feels like kissing flower petals,
purple iris opening slowly to moonlight mouth
revealing the inner layers of ecstasy,
softness enough to whisper seduction
yet scream destruction
all in one,
and she undulates into me,
unrelenting dance to the ocean Gods,

waves of her rock me, rock me, lift me from my foundation,
the tightening and releasing of her muscles,
the pulse of her body,
the arch and crest of her back,
the ebb and flow of her whitecap kiss,
the heat, the electricity,
lightning that flies from my body into hers,
and from hers into mine,
undeniable,
even God would call it beauty being born.

Savoring the sweet curves of her silk,
I dive into her and begin to feel her swell,
she breathes new life into my kisses,
and dances under the direction of my love,
I envelop her in my skin, and love her
inner middle, I deliver a flare and flicker
that makes me want to reconsider
the life I live without her in it.
She breathes in rhythm to my swirls,
wet desire, moist fire, sweeping over us both,
I seduce the woman in her core
to come out of hiding and beg for more,
more from a woman who recognizes her strength,
more from a woman who recognizes her brilliance,
more from a woman who recognizes
the sheer intensity of our desire,
and who just wants to stand naked starlight next to her fire.

Each moment builds,
her body is nearing explosion,
but I am the volcano,

our lava burns us both
and forms new uncharted land between our legs,
where we will live and die by each other's sides,
I devour her sex and dreams,
and wait my whole life for that moment she screams,
sweet release of that which she has bottled in,
nectar of the woman who makes me alive in her skin.

## ⌘ Be Coming

Hold all my aching and growing,
make your body a vessel
for everything I have to fill you,
it may not be much
but it might just be everything.

I have heard the soul is shaped like a bowl
a reversed dome of the Heavens,
we are golden receptors of beauty,
magnets that pull stars into our lowest points
until they build towers of light
from our sternums.

Rise and fall chest,
metronomic movement of body
keeping time for the sages,
inside me a heart breathing
sound of lullabies for sleeping angels,
Great Servers
who wear gravity like a badge of honor,
like a gown of trees rooted in earth,

wake up, my friends,
hold my hand through this;
I think I know the way,
otherwise, my true north tongue
will hasten into Mercury-mouthed stutters of half truths
and I will taste the metal compass spin,
follow my fallen sparred-off feathers
to the gates of your own becoming,

Be coming,
Be going back to that body of light
that birthed you like a sun into space,
the plasma of dreams,
the expectancy of orbits,
the nomenclature of God, who has a thousand names

All of them being You.
All of them being Me.

## ⌘ Planting Stars

I buried a handful
of stars deep into the soil,
scattered diamonds
lighting
everything black,
you know how dirt smells like possibility
when it is just that dirt and your naked fingers?
It's primal.
It's energy.
It's holding something that never ends.
I felt that today.

I will wait to tell you where
I buried the stars,
wait to see if a constellation
can really form
from dust and spit and earthworms and myth.

In a few weeks,
I will go out alone,
no, I will bring you with me,
and we will find an empty space in the night sky,
that all of a sudden becomes a distant tiny sprout of light,
and we will hold our breath,

 waiting to see our reflection.

## ⌘ Tiny Boat

Today,
I am a tiny boat,
on a huge empty ocean,
with nothing but the longing in the wind
looking for someone to push around,
looking for someone to sing to,
and my ears are open,
but I can't recognize the sound.
I hardly try.

Reaching out towards the sky,
the blue fills me
and I become water,
but I still don't know
which way is up
or which way is down.

A side effect of woman is that
I am tied by my heartstrings
to the pull of sea,
and new moons sometimes
open up old wounds
to let the light in.

My heart floats
even if it's heavy.
On some distant horizon,
a woman with a lighthouse
in her chest
is remembering the sound of my name.

I am a tiny boat,
drifting,
high tides shifting on an ocean of grace.
I'll shoot a flare from my bow,
out into the night
and wait for the stars
to notice
that I am gone.

For now,
I am adrift,
ribcage boat frame anchored
to the rising and daunting crescent.

## ⌘ Siren

She lies prostrate beneath
the languid, pale moon chanting desperate
wolf songs to the wind,
I know her skin,
remember the buoyancy of her mouth,
unsinkable ship clawing for a beacon on the water,
shaping lighthouse wishes from the sea's mist,
wanting nothing but homecoming,
nothing but a respite on the open shores of someone's thighs,
this is the woman
that named Jezebel from experience,
that no one recalls in the light of day, her hollow chest
a cacophony of echoes.

In the night,
she welcomes everything that sails
to drop anchor onto her wrists
and have their fill of treasures,
she is not without treasures,
she is the moving waves,
rolling hips, typhoon howl,
it's been too long since she was called Siren
but tonight her ears will no longer bleed,
her song is unforgettable
and asks you to forget all you know,
all at once.

I don't remember, but
maybe I loved her,
maybe I am her.

# ⌘ Constant Before Picture

There is nothing wrong with being
the constant "before" picture,
the widened mirror
that women stand in front of
to judge their own beauty and bigness,
to see that they are the lucky "after" photo,
maybe *after* exercising I could see my feet from up here,
maybe *after* eating better I would not have to roll into the next room,
they are the skinny versions of this obvious whale,
keep your silent snickers and sympathy to yourself
because I have been on both sides of this body.

I was a size 24 and went down to a size 4
in a little over a year,
my friends and family missed the fat me,
the silent, sarcastic sponge,
the stoic statue they could lean on,
the funny one, the wallflower waiting,
they did not know what to do with that much beauty,
but I knew I always had it.

I know I still do.
I am a size 14 now, tipping the scales
back on the side of voluptuous,
because there is too much riding on these bones,
too much light holding this body up
to be that small,
too much fight to be that frail,
you can't hold a fire in a thin straight line
and expect to be warmed,

you must keep it wide and strong,
spread me out to light the villages,
there is more than enough of me to go around.

My body sustains people,
gives life,
my flesh feeds,
glows,
has dreams tucked away in its folds,
pillows the weary heads,
I hold the sun between my hips,
my thick tree trunk thighs
root a lineage of Amazons and volcanoes,
I am too big to be small!
Size 4 cannot hold my charge,
my fire, my passions,
the comets that fire out of my mouth,
the pulsing vibrations of energy from the galactic center
that electrify my spine
and dance like an arrow of flame from the heavens.
You try and put all that Goddess in a tiny shell!

I may look like a "before" picture to you,
but all you have is that so called perfect body;
I hold Heavens inside me,
I carry lifetimes on these beautiful holy feet,
planets are my swollen breasts,
my shoulders hold up the stars,
my monolith head can be seen from space,
ancient temple of olive brown skin,
frankincense smoke in my breath,
each word an escaping blessing,

Before.
Yes, lifetimes *before*.
Yes, ions *before*.
I am a swirling galaxy in human form,
cut me cross section and see the concentric circles of my orbits,
I am an Angel, with clipped wings,
here in this body to help YOU evolve
here in this form so YOU can see yourself.

I hold everything you will never know
in this giant and glorious vessel.

# ⌘ The Way She Walks into the Ocean

I have always loved
the way the she walks into the ocean,
her golden head tilted back,
her arms stretched
like opening wings,
fingers dancing on the undulating horizon,
each step she takes
folds the waves up her legs,
they kiss her hips,
wrap around her body,
the ocean is her sparkling gown.

This is always like witnessing
a coming home,
a holy communion,
like the aching and longing of Penelope
waiting by the shore for Odysseus,
her body prostrate on the sand,
the waves lapping her skin,
her blue eyes, a constant lighthouse,
her tears and the ocean
merging into one.

## ⌘ Sandcastle

I have heard that I build foundations on sand,
on everything that easily washes away,
that there is not solid ground where I stand,
that I hammer nails into water.

Maybe I choose movement
and pliability under my feet because
a rigid house would have already crumbled in these storms,
cobblestone and panic do not mix into beauty,
brick and mortar are strong, yes, but my emotions are fluid,
and only yielding earth holds my moving body.

That may not suit you,
that may not be something you can trust,
but I know that my sand is a fine silt
that glows with flaxen softness,
and that may not be what you are looking for

in a lover,

but I am building a sandcastle from my toes up,
every cell of me, a bed for pearls,
a changeable mountain,
water-packed golden rooms
that absorb the secrets of stars and tides,

bring your heart to this table,
make an offering
but do not set out to test the soundness of my walls,
I will collapse into myself willingly at the thought of challenge
because

there is enough out there to disprove love,
I am not here to be the subject of hypothetical reasoning,
believe in the daylight of my heart,
believe in the castle that holds ground for the ocean to kiss,
believe in the dawn to dawn that I hold the sun for you.

I am building a sandcastle from my toes up,
my foundation is the whole moving, blessed earth,
unbreakable,
eternal.

## ⌘ Abuelita

She sits in the window seat of this mechanical bird,
hunched over,
under a hand-stitched blue blanket draped across her lap,
someone's grandmother,
abuelita del amor,
paper thin caramel skin,
silk turtle shell back,
deep lines tracing journeys on her wise face,
I see her in my mind,
rolling corn and flour
into soft doughy nourishment
between her crookeding fingers,
gently rushing her grandchildren to dress for church,
tortilla hands clutching one another as the plane begins
its slow ascent into the sky.
She is someone's mother, someone's wife,
someone's friend, someone's life,
incapable of translation,
unnecessary because her heart speaks my language,
old spanish eyes that show everything to me,
as I am the only one who cares to really take notice of her.
I look behind her thick, round lenses
and see a woman who is a beacon to her family,
a woman who is the sun to each growing rose,
a woman who has struggled, but did it smiling.
Lines don't lie.
I wonder who she is going to see,
who is waiting to pick her up at the airport.
I would wait for her.
Abuelita.

She makes the sign of the cross, nervously, as we reach the air,
her hands now twiddle, tangle into the thick fibers of her blanket.
I wish I was not so far away from her
so I might soothe her anxiety
with a conversation in my broken Spanish.
Perhaps she would tell me
about her granddaughter getting married in Monteréy,
or about her childhood friend
who suddenly can't remember anything,
or about the way she made breakfast for her husband
everyday for 63 years
and now that he is gone, she always
has too many eggs and chorizos in the fridge.
Perhaps we would laugh
and the lines on her face would transform
into another map of her life,
a connect-the-dot pattern of pure joy.
I smile just thinking of it,
and she sees me smiling from down the row,
and in that moment, neither of us feels alone.

## ⌘ Peace Bombs

If there were peace bombs
would we drop them?
Would we board our fighter planes
and release peace into the atmosphere, the at-most-fear?
The heightened level of anxiety that so many
children have to go to sleep to swimming in?
They don't count sheep,
they count seconds between explosions,
they count lost family members,
they count unnoticed teardrops
and crumbled buildings that used to be schools.
They don't count sheep,
they don't sleep.
They live waking nightmares that
are disguised as revolution and dressed as progress.

If there were peace bombs,
would we stockpile them,
hold them back from the world
and wait for the perfect
and most capitalistically opportune time
to drop them on the Arab Spring
and the Egyptian Evolution
and the Syrian Seizure of Power,
and the Israel vs. Palestine conflict,
and the American war-zones here at home,
where we brandish weapons against each other
and defeat our own people with different skin color,
or would we wait
and just let them devour each other?

Would we forget our transgressions,
dispel our aggressions and see that
HEALING should be our only obsession?
Would we intercede with our peace bombs
and fulfill the need to breathe
a collective sigh of relief
that there won't be the start of World War Three,
because we have peace bombs,
and we will drop them for free?

If there were peace bombs,
I would be all for dropping them,
I would form coalitions
so there would be no hope of stopping them,
the peace bombs
would rebuild cities,
and bring back the dead,
the peace bombs would take back all
the unnecessary bloodshed,
If there were peace bombs,
there would be no more war,
there would finally be ONENESS
and a New World to explore.

If there is a peace bomb,
drop one on me,
because, it's breaking my heart,
that war is all I see.

## ⌘ Open Letter from an Afghan Woman to an American Woman

Do you even know that I have a face under here?
Under these sheets and sheets of fabric
that bind me and hide me,
there is a life, there is a mouth muffled screaming,
I have a body just like you, a mind that wanders, too,
There is no difference between you and me,
I am a woman that just longs to be free.
How can you allow this to happen to us, Dear America?
How can you see these huddled masses of frightened fabric on the
news and not be outraged or saddened by the thought of us?

I lost my baby sister to a stranger yesterday.
He slit her throat with a sacrificial blade,
in front of a crowd of 30 men, and laughed,
laughed at the thought of a woman having a soul,
laughed at the thought of a woman entering an afterlife,
laughed at my dishonorable tears seeping
through the wet blanket of my face.
She was just a little girl, nine years old, giving birth to daydreams,
only to end with her blood staining red forever the silk of my burqa.

What is the point of life under a sheet?
Like a ghost of humanity that no one sees,
A ghost with no thoughts and no words, only silence.
I have no identity, no spirit, ho hope, no life.
I have no will to live anymore, as a shadow in an unforgiving land.
I do not want to be another casualty to the wills of men.
I do not want to be slaughtered in an arena in front of a crowd,
a crowd that brings their wives and daughters to murder,
sisters and mothers, all without faces, all without hope.

We are the women of this forgotten land, this ignored tragedy,
trapped in a sea of cheap silk and head scarves,
forever drawn curtains, veiling our light.
We make a holy room impure with our womanhood.
We corrupt any holy atmosphere of men by our presence.
Why are we so low on this pyramid of life?
Where do our dreams go when we fall asleep?

Here I am dirt, I am spit, I am nothing, always.
My daughters will be nothing, will be dirt.
Their daughters will be nothing, will be dirt.
I must stop this cycle of oppression from thriving,
but I can already feel the hurling stones flying towards me,
their heavy screaming mouths, breaking my bones.
I want to rip out the heart of my sister's killer,
and my mother's killer, and my daughter's killer.
Religion is not justification for continuing this ritual oppression.
Where is my God? America?
These sacrifices and executions for honor must stop.
Can you hear me through this FUCKING MUFFLING FABRIC?!!

Women like me are getting the soul beaten out of them,
usually by the hands of their own husbands or fathers.
Women like me are dying everyday for nothing,
for sacrifice, for honor, for pleasure, for entertainment,
ENTERTAINMENT!!!
Is that not enough to shock you into helping me?
I am going to die if my husband finds this letter.
I should not even know how to write, let alone think,
I should not think like you, American woman, or speak like you,
I have been punished enough times.

I have been brainwashed to think that I deserve to die for this.
Maybe I do deserve to die.

50

Maybe I should just end this suffering and speak out loudly
so the punishment comes
like a quick deadening blow that kills my spirit,
like the spirits of the ghost women before me.
There has to be something better for me after death,
something so wonderful to make up for all this suffering.
There must be a place where my soul can escape,
where I can speak, and read, and think, and laugh.
Oh, what is it like to laugh?
Does it feel like a color?
I want to know,
I want to feel the tightening of my empty belly
in a deep laugh about nothing in particular.
What is freedom like?
Without a robe, hiding my every expression,
my every desire, my every dream.
I once caught a glimpse of myself when I was washing.
It was a reflection off a basin in the sun.
I think I am beautiful.
I want to see myself again,
without this completely enveloping cloth,
losing all my form, my femininity, myself,
underneath this burqa, screaming,
"Let me out!!!
Please, LET ME OUT!!!"

Are there mirrors after death...?
and makeup...?
and smiles…?

## ⌘ From Inside the Tower

My winged heart is in a tower,
I peer through barred tiny window
to see the patch of blue sun,
a breath of sky dancing shadows on the wall,
I become the window,
the overarching stone that lies on the cusp
of inside and out,
of cold and everything that is giving birth as spring,
I become the wall,
kiss my own shadows until they no longer
join my feet and merge into me,
they are free winged things,
circling overhead as a chorus of angels
not serpents,
no, not dark,
not gargoyles that laugh at this delusion,
this tower is a closed mouth,
is a closed cell, and all of my cells are locked inside,
no place to divide, no music of spiritual mitosis spreading
its melodies on the waves of zephyrs,
only stasis, emotional inertia,

the infinite depths of Love
are all that can hear to the deep belly of my cries,
and through the keyhole of the padlock
that holds me in this pensive and sullen eternity,
I can hear the faint roaring of a dragon's breath,
with enough fire to melt
whatever mechanism is keeping me here.

When all illusion
is melted into a liquid gold pool,
and I emerge unscathed,
I see that the tower
was always
my sky-reaching ribcage,
my winged heart
holding every birdsong,
my arms, my hands, unchained and open.

## ⌘ Deconstruction

Deconstruction
lies only in the true
breakdown of that which
constructs the psyche and spirit,
those rods and ropes
and pulleys and stones
that build a soul through experience,
to reflect upon the WHY
of who you really are,
to reflect upon the chaos that
most likely breeds more chaos in you
unless it is identified
and released from within,
to reflect upon the prototypes,
the archetypes
that built us from baby,
to reflect upon the amalgamation
of all moments and life that
construct the NOW,
you must undo
every nail and screw,
untie every lie and truth
and scrutinize with objective eye
every action, reaction, attraction and distraction
that leads your heart and mind astray,
away from the center
of the pure and absolute form,
the true
and quintessential You.

Break down the walls
from the frame and shame
of your bones,
leave no stone unturned
until there is nothing but LIGHT,
blinding, penetrating,
radiating, illuminating LIGHT.

Deconstruction
of the wall of untruth and ego
that shrouds each man,
that veils each woman,
is the only way that our culture, our humanity, our world,
can REBUILD... can SURVIVE.

## ⌘ How a Tree Becomes a Wildflower

A few days ago,
we cut down a huge dead tree,
a dried out Mighty Oak
its empty thick branches reached high into the night,
blocking out whole constellations with its sprawling,
a mangled sore thumb eyesore to cars driving by,
until it came down with a wailing, "TIMBERrrrrrrrrr......."
and an explosive, echoing thud.
Horizon of evergreen pines getting sunspace and
the autumn color palette taking back the view,
a little more sky,
open.

Massive fragments of limbs shattered,
meeting earth from the clouds.
Yes, oak shatters.

We cut up the fallen giant into logs,
french bread loaf slices of tree,
each log about eighteen inches long,
fireplace size,
hundreds of them,
enough warmth for ten winters.

I filled the Jeep with logs,
made stacks and stacks by the house to keep dry.

I went to the hardware store,
bought a new ax,
or technically a log splitter,
because the handle on the last one broke in half

in the felling of giants,
the new one is a 6-pound maul splitter,
resemblant viking ax with moon-shaped blade
on one side of the head, blunt heaviness on the other.

I had no idea, a couple of years ago,
that I would be living in the country,
splitting logs with a giant ax,
halving and quartering and halving again,
stacking piles of neatly fallen wood soldiers into
how warm will we be when the mercury dips
below freezing tomorrow?

There is a primal feeling about it all,
a pioneer spirit that is woven through the fibers,
the shedding of bark that smells like forest,
the concentric circles of growth that I am splitting like atoms,
the sound of what wood sounds like dividing in half
and falling by the strength of my swing,
by the drive of my aim,
the vibration going through my hands and up my arms,
the energy released as I exhale
and I see the breath of cold air biting back at my cheeks,
the numbness of my fingers setting in,
I keep chopping, splitting.

It is all cyclical.
This is what going back to the source looks like.
My left arm becomes a cradle for split logs,
firewood load that I bring up to the porch
and put in the basket outside by the door,
the basket of split logs and kindling that is fireplace bound,
the spirit of trees that will keep us warm tonight.

The logs sing a song of crackling when they burn,
sometimes they whistle,
not quite cured for perfect burning
but warm just the same.
As the flames dance around the sticks and split logs,
I thank them for what they give,
what they have given,
for the life that they lived as a tree,
and for the ashes that they will become.

Tomorrow we will shovel the ashes out of the fireplace
and put them in a bucket with the few twigs that did not burn.
We will dump the ashes back onto the earth,
after a couple of days,
the ashes of split logs will become one with the dirt,
they will fertilize the dirt
that will birth wildflowers come Spring.

This is what going back to the source looks like.

## ⌘ Meditation on a Canoe

I became the sun today,
closed my eyes and burst into flame,
melted the canoe I floated in and sank into the water,
a steaming fireball descending into blue and green,
a thousand minnows warmed their silver bodies
by my sizzling and bubbling inferno,
their iridescent underwater kaleidoscope of frenzied swimming
made me forget this was a dream.

I am Icarus,
unyielding to the warnings of my father,
melted wax covered brown body,
tar and feathers and pride,
I would feed my hubris to the fish,
turn their tiny mouths into flames, but this too
is chimera biting my earlobes.
There is no way to silence your thoughts if you are trying.
Do flies have ears? because if so,
how can they stand the noise of their own flying?
Maybe if I just think of the color blue,
or an empty jar,
or the sky,
of flight, not of falling.

When the wind moves me softly across
the water's surface, I finally feel weightless,
as the cacophony of thoughts
write poems about themselves in my head,
a doubled looping chorus,
 implosion.

## ⌘ Red Balloon Heart

This is what I would say to you,
these are the letters that would somehow make up my love,
these are the sounds that I would cry-out-belly into the wind to you,
that would color outside the lines of my body and find the curves
where you begin, and where you end,
this is my crescendo, love,
this is the song that I never wrote
but I hear in my head when I remember
that it was you who makes music in making love, black notes
climbing the lines of my ribcage staff like a ladder
transcendent scales to my mouth,
tuning fork strike my bones
and dance to my vibration hum,
this is that song, and the silences of breath sounds between,
the rhythm of building and destroying and building again,
this is the helium hope that floats
my red balloon heart to sky-grabbing hand
that clutches the air for my string,
this is my string - hold it close to your heart,
don't let go,
I tried the wind, but I prefer your safe,
you save me every second you know me,
just by knowing me how you do,
pull me closer, love,
release my air into your mouth and fill up your chest with my love,
make your voice a few octaves higher with my exhale,
inhale, don't fail me now, love,
sing a high pitched song,
so high that dogs perk their ears up and know
that you are calling me home.

## ⌘ Glow

You broke a glow stick
in a blurred dance on the lawn,
splattered the glowing drops
onto your shirt, your back, your shoes,
your chest, whipping the bright blue-white
onto your body, your hands,
still dancing, splashing so much light.
You looked like the Heavens,
like a blanket of night stars,
collected constellations
swaying in front of me,
like I could reach out and
touch a moving universe.

# ⌘ Orion

I contemplated Orion tonight,
perched high at the midpoint of night,
stretching out his arms and legs into infinity,
one, two, three belted perfection,
Kings in a line.
How is it,
out of all those stars,
in all that seeming chaos and frenzied light,
in all that expanse of untouchable space,
how is it,
that there is that one, two, three
perfect line of light
in the winter's night sky?
The evenly spaced ellipsis written by the hand of God,
an unfinished thought . . .
a wait, there is more to come . . .
a star sentence that trails off into silence . . .

⌘ This is how to eat your past:

go to that place where you keep it,
maybe it is dark there,
find it,
your past,
yes, the one you try not to look at,
the one you try to grow up from,
not claim,
exclaim,
compare things to,
analyze,
hate analyzing,
use as an excuse,
try to forget.
Take it,
hold it between your fingers and thumb,
put it between your teeth and bite down
just to make sure it is real and hardened,
a golden piece of you,
lack-luster lust,
shocked by moments,
packed with triggers,
unpack it,
lay everything out across the kitchen table
under the cheap chandelier that never stops swaying,
in the solitude of this necessary digestion,
compartmentalize the moments of bliss and disaster,
tears from laughter,
separate,
make piles,
pour yourself a glass of chilled vodka from the freezer,

drink it,
keep compartmentalizing,
look at each moment under the light
of right now and see if it shines or not,
see what pulls out the demons
that are stuffed inside,
illumine the silenced desires,
chase down the bitter pills with sweet,
find the bitter,
find the hurt,
separate the brighter moments from darker ones,
find the I wish I could just forget ones,
find the "I'd rather ignore this pile of
everything that makes me cry,"
find the day your Daddy drove away after
leaving you and mommy and sister in another country,
find learning the word divorce,
find worrying and fear,
find the day at 13 when you were raped
by the dark hands of a stranger,
how the stranglehold of silence
held you for five years with a secret
you were too ashamed to tell your mother,
find every time someone called you a fucking dyke,
find your first girlfriend telling you how she wished
you were a man so you could get married,
find losing her too soon,
find the mistake of joining the corps of cadets,
find the hazing because you were a girl
trying to drum with men and they hated you for it,
find the bruises and the yelling,
find the jolting alarm clock of men yelling at your face,
find them foaming at the mouth with misdirected rage,
find marching in full winter dress uniform

for hours and hours in the scorching heat
as a punishment for not voting for George W. Bush,
find Don't Ask, Don't Tell military,
find the public humiliation of getting kicked out
for loving a girl that never told,
(take a moment to thank the Universe that you escaped that hell),
find every time your next girlfriend
wouldn't hold your hand in public,
or tell anyone she was with you,
find how she was embarrassed of how fat you were,
put that up to the light,
see what shines through,
there will be shining,
there will be rust,
find the wreckage,
find the war-torn,
find the broken pieces that you have hidden away for so long,
or tucked so far down in your chest
that you almost forgot they were there.
Take all of those moments and collect them in your hands,
they will feel like shards of glass,
jagged pieces of yourself,
a stained glass window explosion,
squeeze them,
turn them to water,
let the water run through your fingers
taste it,
taste it becoming growth,
be quenched by anything that's left,
see the water as a safe place to be born,
you won't forget what hurt,
but now you will not bleed as you swallow.

There is another pile of moments,
with the night comes the promise of dawn,
find the smiles now, not so broken one,
find the calm in all that thunder,
find the softness,
find the pleasure,
find the laughter,
find what looks like the first time you were kissed,
at 18, when she leaned over and kissed you,
it was your birthday, remember?
after months of you loving her and finally
she answered your lips with yes,
taste that moment,
find that young innocent love
that made you sneak out in the middle of the night,
drive an hour to her house,
climb through her window she left cracked open for you,
and kiss each other so much your stomachs ached,
find leaving just before sunrise,
driving home filled with her scent on your clothes,
how *chloe narcisse* perfume still makes your knees weak,
find that bliss,
swallow it down so it lights up your insides,
turns your belly into a lamppost
that lights the streets of your shadows,
turns your throat into a lighthouse
that guides your heart home,
find all the moments that taste like honeysuckle,
or feel like dewdrops,
or sound like hummingbird wings,
or make you believe there is heaven,
find seeing your students learn to love writing
because you taught them,
find speaking your mind and not being afraid

that the truth you know will make you lose someone,
find how a woman loved your body when you hated it,
how she caressed every big curve as a supple garden and made you
love yourself,
find knowing yourself,
find discovering Infinity,
find that moment you felt ONE with the Universe,
find the moonlight canoe ride under the stars with her,
find making love on the sands of an ocean shore
at midnight under a watchful moon,
find riding a horse on that same shore the next day like a warrior
and feeling liberation bounding through your thighs,
waves crashing and the heat of the day rising from your skin,
collect those moments,
yes all of them,
moments such as this we'll call Beauty,
take all that Beauty,
it maybe looks like diamonds
or a handful of stars,
see it in all of its shimmering glory,
reflecting galaxies and moon shine and firelight
in all of its magnificence,
and yes,
swallow that, too,
let it become you.

Eat all of the gleaming.

Eat all of the gleaming.

## ⌘ Breaking Point

Everything has a point of reachable breaking,
a star has to die before we see its light,
day breaks through night
to bloom sun on morning's mouth,
each of us weary
fragile walkers of earth has a tipping point
that we cannot see until everything around
us is blown into a million pieces,
illusion denies rationality,
tenderness is defied,
communication becomes a black box
never found,
and no one is searching,
a pinprick in what was perfection
implodes, folds in on itself,
black hole vacuum,
and there is nothing I can do to stop
the runaway train
that is my own broken shell
masquerading as truth.

Do you see this happening in your life?
Have you swallowed your own shadow?
Witnessed your own loss of control?
A slow motion chaos dance,
tunnel vision into darkness from light,
the music... stopping.
Everything slipping away while you
sit on your hands, screaming.
Breaking points can be left as just that,
Broken.

Shards of self clinging to destruction,
instigating carnage,
loss,
forgetting,
damning everything to hell,
tearing apart foundations built with conscious hands.

Breaking points can also be breaking through,
breaking open,
breaking out of old form,
stepping outside of the mountain
of emotional anarchy rising inside
and planting a red flag of defiance against the
raging of your own demons,
step outside of the whirlpool
and see your body from outside of it,
float above.

You have your own set of brakes.
You are equipped with Spirit
enough to hold in the falling apart.
Let go of the not self that graffitis empty promises
on the inner walls of your psyche,
and reach out for calm,
skylight your head center,
enter the clouds,
remember the hands you sit on are also Wings,
reach out for a friend that holds your heart like a newborn,
reach out for the light of your own pulsing beauty,
see the fiery Soul that walks with you into every step,
that higher reflection of all your broken glass,
the God in you that is in the throes of your
BECOMING.

You are not broken.

You are not broken,
you are breaking out,
you are breaking open,
you are breaking through.

# ⌘ A Ladder and Butterflies

A ladder
leading up
to a humble swarm of
golden origami butterflies
dangling staggered from invisible strings,
different heights,
a flock of marigolds
in flight
dancing in a delicate spray,
whisper for me to notice.

The elementals of dreams
sometimes give glimpses
to the physical world,
mundane things beg to slip into the surreal,
to become the feast and not the fetters,
to remind us that the lines are blurred,
the wall between worlds
is merely a rice paper screen,
a mirage of shadows
from either side.

## ⌘ On Writing

Profound.
Something Divine.
Profound, I haven't found yet,
but I know the expectation is there,
the waiting on my words to flower into a lotus
of understanding and insight,
but tonight, I just feel like going back to look at
my older poems, retyping them,
reigniting them into who I am today,
because all of those words
built a foundation for my cracked book spine,
every word saved my life at some point
and yes, looking back at them,
I see how much I was hurt,
but now I see how much I have grown,
how my words don't really sting anymore,
they sing.

I cannot pressure myself into
following some sort of expectation.
Maybe I don't want to write about galactic openings
and alignments, and the way the planet standing next to me
is louder than I would care to listen to.
I don't like loud.
I shiver.
I drown.
Loud makes me want to run away.
I want quiet.
I want calm.

I want to hear ripples on a glass-surfaced lake
dancing from the solitary pebble I drop into it,
and those ripples finally reaching a shore
that I couldn't remember until now.
My words can save me tonight, if I let them.
They can be my waiting life raft,
they can be my quickly sinking ship,
they can be my disaster splattered all over an empty page,
or they can be my finding,
my being found,
my no longer lost,
song.

# ⌘ กรุงเทพมหานคร Bangkok

1.

Nothing of Bangkok
resounds in my bones,
no smells,
no sounds,
no images etched onto the rice paper of my memory,
the passing light
of Gleaming Golden Imperial Dragon Barges
gliding down the murky central khlong,
the dirty river marketplace of softened produce
sold from leathered old women in congested tiny boats.
The Golden Barges of the King making waves,
rocking the floating fruit huts, souring in the heat.

Nothing of this is from my memory,
I am putting together pieces as I write,
and creating a scene in my mind
that is dressed like a memory,
but Bangkok may as well be Alaska
cold in its un-remembrance,
like I was never even there,
like I was not born at
โรงพยาบาลจุฬาลงกรณ
(King Chulalongkorn Memorial Hospital)
on the first day of the year,
on the first year of the decade,
the first child in a marriage that held desperately to lasting.

2.

Trauma does funny things to memory.
Inserts clouded grey areas,
Sometimes over whole years.
Loses connections to colors,
but I know from pictures that I wore a
different colored gingham print dress to school every day,
Monday was green, or Tuesday blue,
I know for sure Friday was yellow,
I always loved the yellow one because
the yellow and white blended into sunshine
and didn't look so... gingham,
and Friday was yellow, or Thursday,
and my face looks so happy,
I can almost smell the rust on those monkey bars,
but don't remember that I could climb them.

3.

When Bangkok was ripped
out of my seven-year-old hands
and my father went away with my country,
I dropped all my memories out of a tiny hatch
in the airplane headed for America,
just let them slip from my tiny fingers,
underneath my oversized seat,
each one falling through the life preserver,
through the cold cloud-covered metal of the airplane belly
and into the oblivion of sky and the widest ocean I have ever seen,
but don't remember seeing.

## ⌘ That Day I was Jesus Christ
## (Total Eclipse of the Heart)

When I think of eclipses,
I remember a skit I was in where I played the part of Jesus,
yes, Jesus Christ,
hanging on a cross
in front of 2,000 people,
a chubby girl - almost a woman,
a closeted young maybe lesbian,
an inner confusion and desperate sadness,
arms stretched out,
hands grasping the back of the mighty crossbar,
breasts holding, softly, the word "MESSIAH"
written boldly in neon green on a white t-shirt.

I was 17,
a tomboy with no makeup
baggy torn bluejeans,
sarcasm lingering on my lips,
dark hair that curtained each side of
my sullen, stoic face.
It was the hair that hung in front of my face
that set me apart from the other kids
in my Catholic church youth group,
as we prepared to perform this skit at a conference
where 2,000 kids would gather to worship,
and I was mostly a tangled mess
of not belonging everywhere,
and feeling this "God" might be a safe place,
or at least less dark than alone with my thoughts.
Plus, my mom made me go.

So there I was,
making my lesbian Jesus debut,
I held in the laughter, I think,
maybe didn't even realize the irony until years later,
swallowed the stage-fright, chased it with a little terror.

The skit was a dramatization
set to the song...
you guessed it, *Total Eclipse of the Heart*
yes, "*turn around...*
*every now and then I get a little bit blah, blah, blah, blah...*"
that's the one.
Got the song in your head?
Good.

Here I am, Jesus,
standing on the tiny platform,
arms and body hanging on a thick wooden cross,
brown curtained face looking down
as the other kids slyly vulture around the heroine of the skit,
a pretty, popular girl being taunted
by all the pressures of growing up,
the personifications of evil sins and dangerous vices
circling her, prodding her, screaming in her face
SEX (circling)
ALCOHOL (circling)
WEED (circling)
COCAINE (circling)
ECSTASY (circling)
LYING (circling)
SKIPPING CLASS (circling)
STEALING (circling)
PREGNANCY (circling)
DROPPING OUT (circling)

Around and around,
around and around some more,
faster and faster, (it almost makes me cringe)
these walking taunting posters of so-called sins
surround our young heroine
in a sea of hopelessness and despair,
until finally, she crashes to the ground in total loss!
Through the silence sings
the bellowing raspy voice of Bonnie Tyler...

*"Turnaround bright eyes, but every now and then I fall apart!*
*Turnaround bright eyes, every now and then I fall apart!*
*And I need you now tonight!*
*And I need you more than ever!*
*And if you only hold me tight!*
*We'll be holding on forever...*
*I really need you tonight! Forever's gonna start tonight..."*

That's when I step off the cross
and to go to her,
my broken young follower,
my torn down, persecuted child,
as if I am Savior,
as if I am Messiah,
Mess i ah,
Mess I am,
Mess of me becoming salvation?

At that moment, I almost believe it,
the 2,000 sets of hopeful eyes moved by the chaos,
the dramatic lighting,
the whirling and screaming
suddenly stopped by this brief tenderness,

we all wanted to be saved like this
we all wanted that hanging story of a man to be a friend,
a real and tangible God.

*"I really need you tonight!*
*Forever's gonna start tonight!*
*Forever's gonna start tonight!*
*Once upon a time there was light in my life*
*But now there's only love in the dark"*

I went to her and pulled her up into my arms,
I held her in the most believable way,
and wrapped her in everything that I could muster
that looked like Strength,
that looked like picking up pieces of shattered life,
that looked like Jesus Christ reaching out His compassionate hand,
through my own trembling, troubled 17 year old fingers,

*"Nothing I could say, a total eclipse of the Heart*
*Turnaround bright eyes, every now and then I fall apart*
*Turnaround bright eyes, every now and then I fall apart"*

She looked at me like I was someone else,
not the same girl that made jokes at rehearsal,
as tears poured down both of our faces,
and I looked out to a sea of many young eyes welling,
it was as if something came through me,
even I believed in my own power
for that moment,
I held her again and the spotlight
made it appear that we were both glowing.
I took her hand and we went to each of the kids holding the posters,
each frozen in their places after her collapse,

*"Turnaround, every now and then I get a little bit terrified*
*And then I see the look in your eyes*
*Turnaround bright eyes, but every now and then I fall apart*
*Turnaround bright eyes, every now and then I fall apart"*

They dropped their signs as I embraced them,
"sex, alcohol, weed, cocaine, ecstasy, lying, skipping class,
stealing, pregnancy, dropping out"
like falling leaves on the stage floor,
their characters rushing to my arms
like I was offering some blanket of forgiveness,
and maybe I was.

I walked off the stage like I was floating,
they all followed like disciples,
the audience was a roaring hallelujah,
and this was not supposed to be a religious poem,
but God damnit,
I believed in something that day,
maybe it was because those kids believed that I should be Jesus
that something Divine took me over,
maybe I am reimagining this moment more glorious
than it really was, and it was just a skit,
and that was that, end of story,

or maybe it was my very own inner Light
telling me that this was not the only time
in my life that I was to be crucified,
and that those sins would all hold my name
in their hungry mouths.

I don't know…
but I did meet my first girlfriend at that youth conference,
and to this day, every time I hear
Total Eclipse of the Heart,
or I think of eclipses,
I remember a day when I was both broken and Holy,
when I was a mess and a Messiah.
*"Turn around bright eyes..."*

## ⌘ Ode to my Bellybutton

Oh, muffled hole of belly
where have you been the past few years?
I can't see you when I look down anymore,
hidden in the lapping over
of mountainous flesh and folds,
rising hemispheres.

Every time I look in the mirror naked,
my torso is a sad face made from creases and lines,
how my body defines feeling, expresses grief,
nipples as eyes and sad mouth belly button that stretches
into a downward arc of abandon.

I would fear the dark or suffocation
if I had your unfortunate real-estate on my body,
but you have been there since day one,
like a loyal friend,
leftover scar,
umbilical depth of womb wonder and growth,
severance from mother's delivery of everything that I am,

oh, holy hole,
saddened space that is really the birthplace
of all that makes me beauty,
you live in secluded silence,
flattened, quieted mouth,
stretch-mark river-lets that lead to an unseen ocean,
makeshift hipline that crosses your face,
where the tightening of pants
becomes a gag order,

and you would never tell
because our discomfort is shared.

Concealed in the center,
navel wanting light, inward pointing star
that continues to nourish me
from some invisible source,
pulls me to my own core where there is nothing but stillness
and the vibration of planets humming,
orbiting around the fountainhead, the nucleus I call
you, belly button, circle on my body's terrain that never ends
but was always, the beginning.

## ⌘ Pomegranate

I had never eaten a pomegranate by myself,
never granted that luxury to my mouth,
felt that tang in my cheeks
that comes from remembering,
but I took that luxury all for myself
a couple of nights ago when I saw it there,
a solitary glowing red orb,
a pomegranate,
shining in the almost empty light-green fruit bowl,
next to an Anaheim pepper and a clove of garlic.

I didn't even put it on a plate,
just sliced through it with a butcher knife,
cross-section right on the kitchen counter.
It split swiftly like an open heart,
and its juices left a puddle of red underneath the rocking halves,
a sticky trail of my unfamiliarity with this fruit
spreading thin across the clean marble.
Again, I sliced one of the halves and held it in my hand,
examining the tender textures of the skin
and the spongy white insides that encase the tiny red treasures.

I chose a small spoon to dig out the pomegranate seeds.
It did not work.
Neither did a small fork.
My hands... my hands knew what to do.
I sat by the fire and began to unearth the juicy jewels that
hid in pockets of sponginess,
one by one, I unlocked the sponge's grip on the red gems
and popped them into my mouth,
explosions of sweet and sour juices

and the crunch of the inner seeds
propelled me into a lifetime long ago,
the music and sounds and tastes of ancient Persia
resounded in my chest as I fondled
each pomegranate seed between my fingers.
I was there again,
each seed reigniting the distant flame of memory,
of lovers and firesides,
and the strings of sitars
vibrating the forgotten chorus of God chords inside me.
A subtle red stained my lips and fingertips
as they gingerly pulled out the magical kernels.
I recalled the ancient tedious process of women's beauty
in dying my lips pomegranate kissable
and my fingers with a pulsing glow of sinew and riches.

I peeled back the deep red skin to reveal
rows and rows of exposed garnet jewels
that I gathered into falling,
the plate waiting to catch the bounty, on my lap.
Harvest of red raindrops, like distant muffled drumbeats
echoing in the whirlwind of remembrance.

As I excavated each seed,
I could taste the pomegranate's sacred legacy,
painted in the hands of the Virgin Mary,
whispered from the forgotten tombs of Phoenicians,
bellowed in the laughter of Ancient Greeks
dancing drunk around the temples,
intoxicated by the mysticism of this Divine fruit.

I know why the nightingale sings on the pomegranate tree
outside Romeo and Juliet's love-making window;
because their hearts are exposed jewels of beauty and sacrifice,

and the nightingale is the harbinger of dreams.

With each pomegranate seed I eat,
it is like planting a seed inside my belly,
the red, fleshy jewels earthing themselves in my spongy insides,
hidden stories, ancient paintings, distant music,
forbidden fruit, growing roots inside me,
branching out into visions of lifetimes dyed crimson.

My skin is tender.
Excavate me.

# ⌘ If I Could Harvest Moons

If I could harvest moons,
my eyes would understand the meaning of the seasons
that signal the tides rising into floods,
and the reasons that my warrior heart
is flying skyward to search for the answers I left myself
in the caverns of many moon-shadows, lifetimes ago.

If I could harvest moons,
I would take the half-read books out of my worn out satchel
so I could use it for full-moon collecting;
It has an open mouth and knows how to hold Ancient treasures.
I'd hoist my empty moon hammock onto my shoulder,
and walk out in the direction of the horizon tonight... alone.
Moon harvesting is a solitary practice
that takes patience and precise timing.
You have to know the exact moments
to pluck the glowing spheres
of bright light ripeness from the waiting night sky,
as they slowly rise over rolling hilltops edges,
and crest atop crashing ocean waves,
and stand nobly over ancient ruins,
and knowingly illumine the pyramids, all seeing eye in the sky.
I'd harvest all of these moons tonight,
pluck this moon when a couple has their first kiss under it,
that's what makes it ripe,
and this one out of the skinny dipper's sky,
yes, it has just the right taste of flight,
and turn on an extra streetlight for the alley dancers
as they moonlight dance without a bright full moon tonight.

I catch these moons when they are just ready for the picking,
so that they are still fresh
when I package the harvested beauties
for luminescent distribution
to those who live always in the dark, and sigh lonely into cold.
Tonight, the moons make my body dance,
pulling me with their gravity,
pulling the water in me
like a thousand oceans,
making waves inside me
that sound like Heaven breathing,
gravity shifting between earth
and all these moons and earth again,
my feet floating up to tippy-toes as the gentle orbs
fill my satchel, bountiful harvest of Light,
a cluster of levitating moons like balloons glowing in flight.

## ⌘ Abandoned Seeds

On the westernmost tip of Africa,
in the republic of Senegal,
there is a village surrounded
by ocean and desert and forest,
a land of contradictions and secrets,
of ritual and initiation,
a terrain of beaten spirits,
where women walk in circles
with clipped wings and dragging feet,
broken before blooming,
dust storms rising
up to an unforgiving sky,
holding questions like, "what did I do to deserve this?"
and, "somebody please tell me, why?"

The full moon hesitantly rises
knowing it is the impetus for barbarism,
knowing that when it reaches high in the African night,
there will be a different kind of howling.

The women of the tribe gather
their daughters, from babies to teenagers,
and walk across the empty desert,
across the Gambia river
and into the Casamance region
where there is a lush, green canopy of trees
that can muffle the sounds
of ritual tyranny
being passed down like a gift.

They reach the sacred forest,
the soil is rich with blackness,
almost purple it's so black,
blood-dirt mixture of earth,
where the clitoris
of a 7 year old girl,
is

      cut

off
and left buried
in the ground
like an abandoned      seed,
and then another's           seed... seed... seed... seed... seed...
until the forest floor becomes a garden of loss.

Her budding seed is stolen in the night,
by the hands of her own tribeswomen,
in the name of ritual,
in the name of initiation,
in the name of tradition
religion, superstition, womanhood, ignorance and fear,
and because her mother's mother
littered this same forest with skin and screaming.
Millions of seeds severed and scattered over time,
disembodied with dull blades by guilty, guilty hands.

On this night, maybe three dozen girls are cut,
mothers pushing young backs to unforgiving dirt,
legs held open, under a moon that cannot close its eyes.

I can only imagine the color that the soil becomes
when mixed with that much blood,
the hollow scream of a clitoris falling in the forest,
where other women pretend not to hear the sound… of grief.
The young girl is sewn closed,
leaving only two holes,
sewn closed as tribal songs and incantations
lull her into a state of surrender.
Her legs are tied together to keep her from moving,
and she must lay there on her back
underneath the moon for two weeks,
while her emptiness becomes a painful scar,
a sacred ground of betrayal,
a question never asked or answered.

A tribesman will not marry an uncut woman.
An uncut woman is seen as a whore,
an insatiable sex-monger,
unwanted and unclean.

She will not be worth the ox and sheep
that her father will accept as dowry.
She will be shunned in the village
and live a life of solitude and desperation.

For hundreds of years,
spanning countless countries and tribes
this practice has carried on,
passed down as ceremonial certainty
from mothers to daughters,
as natural and necessary to life
as learning to walk, or fetching the water, or skinning a goat.

In 2012, the United Nations General Assembly
passed a worldwide resolution
to ban all forms of Female Genital Mutilation,
classifying it as a human rights violation and child abuse,
and hopefully the woman of Senegal, Africa
have heard the declaration,
have put down their dulled blades,
and let the full moon rise
without the need to plant anymore tender stolen seeds.

This is not a geography lesson, though,
that is to say, there are millions of women living all over the world
that have been robbed of the mountaintop of their sexual pleasure.
There are thousands of girls that still do not understand
what was taken from them and why.
Senegal is not the only land that cuts off unripened fruit.

I write this poem
as a hand reaching out to the broken,
I plant my words
next to their abandoned seeds,
next to the holy spring buds
blooming on the floor of the sacred forest
that took something so sacred to them.
I stand under the lush canopy
and listen for the signs of healing,
a cool breeze,
a river joining the ocean,
a bird's distant song.
I visualize an invisible wall around the forest,
where no one with a dull blade
or backward cultural intentions may enter.

I stand in the light of my words,
to free what is buried in the darkness,
to sing a song for the women that have survived,
as they live their lives, as they birth their babies,
as they flourish into who they have the strength to become.

I light a circle of fire underneath a full moon,
and see them all with phoenix wings,
rising from the ashes of broken,

into

Goddess.

## ⌘ Escaping Our Water

The thickened sky breaks open,
releases everything she has had held in her bosom,
forgets, again, to thank the sun,
forgives the moon's gentle pulling,
and cloudburst cries out the names of all that have risen
into her nameless depths,
into her immeasurable expanses,
cracked open chest of heavens,
deluge of rumbling firmament unleashing
the water of recycling souls.

Humans are 50-65% water,
our earthly bodies holding pulsing oceans,
babies are 75% water,
we are born wet, moving puddles,
constantly rushing rivers ever-toiling toward
the ocean of all that we know as Gods,
yet struggling in the whirling eddies of all that we lack as humans,

and when we escape this matter and return to spirit,
when we transition into death and our souls start another cycle,
when we return to our holy tattered wings,
we rise into the clouds, invisible dancing water,
evaporating from the seething fires
of everything glorious and devastating on earth,
evanescing vapor, distillation of spirits.
Maybe we are just water and soul,
inside only ocean and
weightless consciousness that holds us up
through this blink we call life.

Maybe when the sky breaks her chest wide open,
when thunderous rumbling and lightning
are woven in a torrent of down-pouring water,
there are winged beings
ascending,
slipping up through a heavenly sieve,
their earthly vessels are no longer chains,
are no longer gilded cages they pretend to fly in,
the water of their holy bodies escaping from clouds
into our cupped-together hands.

## ⌘ Jumping

It is no wonder
that a part of you still lives inside me,
in the hollowed out trunk of a tree
that holds my heart,
where your name is carved
in the splintered wood,
and there, a little bird sings our favorite songs
by The Cure and R.E.M. into the night,
like she is calling her lover to come home,
because "Everybody Hurts"...
but home is a memory that she can't get back to,
like childhood fleeting,
like forever down-streaming into unrecognizable surroundings,
the way life quickly takes you,
like choices that form trenches between outreaching hands,
and after a while, you just stop reaching.

I knew I loved you.
I did not know how to love you,
how to hold so much LIFE in my hands.

When we met as teenagers,
I did not know what yearning was,
I had not had a fire placed in my chest yet
for anything except denying my love for girls,
a pretending charade,
a cover-up game that I was no good at playing,
a lie that was only hidden
until one saw the longing in my eyes...
and then there was you,

and your friendship that colored me golden,
and your wild heart that told me stories of a future
with dream-come-trues brimming over
the cup of my shaking hands,
and that passion in your aged-young mouth
speaking tongues of new truth,
and my nine-layered wings that sprouted
because you taught me to jump from the cliff.
You taught me young love,
and what love meant,
and what love could be,
though we never loved each other,
not like that,
not in the way we thought of loving each other
in the hypotheticals and what-ifs of the mind's runaway trains,
but your chest was my sanctuary, your hands, my coming home.

And when I thought you were dying,
and when I thought you had died,
I never wanted to know what happened,
because losing you was "Losing My Religion,"
was losing a foundation that we had built on stars
before our young, eager hearts met,
and I sank into the warmth of knowing you,
and calling you friend.
I lived with losing you
when you were never lost.
I fell in love with a woman,
and she was my first love,
because you loved me first
and gave me the courage to let my eyes talk for my wanting.
I lost her, but never lost what you gave me.

You.

I always held you there,
in that hollowed out trunk of a tree
that holds my heart,
and every time I fall in love,
I run my hands across the splintered wood of your name,
and remember

jumping.

# ⌘ End in Light

*A Ghazal*

Every footstep on the ancient wise path is worth the fight.
There is no other true purpose in life than to end in light.

Deviation is normal - not every journey starts out right,
but there is an internal compass steering to end in light.

Truth blindness and deaf ears defeat your heart's flying,
everything is open - the source begins and ends in light.

Your first heartbeat is a star being born in the blackness.
Each beat and breath brings you closer to ending in light.

I have lived through the chaos of becoming illumined,
shedding false skins and shells, screaming to end in light.

This can be a dancing of spirit if your heart can break through,
be the ever virgin song that aches to fulfill the ending in light.

Life is a burning ground, a filling of a chalice that you hold inside.
My dear, fledgling soul - death is not the only way to end in light.

Let go of what you have been forced to believe is your self,
become everything that you know you are, that bends in light

and is not broken, but transforms into prisms and eleven rainbows,
and knows "I AM" becomes everything you are that ends in light.

## ⌘ We Are, I AM

So many times in my life,
I have screamed an unquenchable longing
into the darkness of a night with no name,
a longing to uncover
the beginning,
the end,
the nonexistence of either,
the completeness of incompletion,
the being complete in everything that is and is not,
I longed for the Truth about all things,
and longed for an answer that requires no words.

A longing like this does not let me sleep
when the whole world is sleeping,
when talk of souls meets rolling eyes and closed minds,
this longing is consciousness
opening like a flower bud into springtime air,
this longing continuously shakes
the fog of numbness and pain
from the veiled windows of my eyes,
and shows me that
I AM, in fact, Awake.

My purpose is a Torch,
a glowing flame on the planet of too much suffering.
My struggle is a Beacon,
a lighthouse beam into the darkness of an empty ocean's night.
My heart is a Rainbow,
prismatic in reflections of understanding that pour
from its bent-backward arch across the blue sky morning.

My eyes are Supernovas,
seeing through to the quintessence in each body holding a soul.

I know your vessels,
I know what chaos looks like,
I know the calm also comes after a storm,
I know the bodies don't fit sometimes,
it is easy to clothe yourself in everything that ever hurt,
I know it is not easy, but let it go,
shed your skins,
regenerate,
let it go,
cooperate with all that is pulsing around you
in the symbiotic dance of light and dark,
the marriage of opposites,
the eternal story that you are writing yourself into,
the journey of your everliving soul,
the black and white checkered floor
that leads to a door,
open it,
come back again and stand in my smile,
bend the bars around your heart,
it is worth it, to finally FEEL.
FEEL ME.
My feet have walked this path many times,
my soles remember the stones
and the places where the oceans meet.
I have been tide-swept into greatness,
but don't think I haven't almost died drowning.
My hands come together to form infinity
because my body is a closed circuit
and I am made of light.

My drumbeat chest recognizes the rhythms
in the steps of my fellow travelers,
children of the stars,
lovers of the moon,
keepers,
seers,
doers,
we meet again,
and again, dear friends,
another day, another life, I remember you without words.

Our lives are how we know each other.
Our lips and tongues speak in flames.
Our eyes have seen the horizon of a world in the making.
We are synonymous with Light.

We are, I AM.

We are, I AM.

# ⌘ From the Edge of a Black Hole

I am speaking sounds into the universe
from    the    edge    of    a

### BLACK HOLE

a dream in a  v a c u u m ,
My body stretches across a mathematical anomaly,
straddles the cusp of the inescapable event horizon,
the absorption of any and all matter and light,
black-hole-speak for point of no return.

Not even the gravitational pull
of my Jupiter Heart
can save the stars whizzing by into nothingness,
beams of fire that fade into
the cosmic silence of this gaping black mouth,
bodies of light that lose the properties that make them light,
once they are pulled into the threshold of the horizon,
the "black hole information loss paradox."

My moonbeam hands pull at the tides of space
but cannot pull the light
out of this massive stellar consumption,
the chaos and symmetry
of a universe folding in on itself,
the bending of planetary trajectories,
the swallowing of stars,
the digestion of milky firmament,
the arcing of covenants,
God's Laws revealing their inconsistencies and delicate imbalance.

I do not get pulled in completely,
my bodies s t r e t c h
but I have my own orbit,
merely a phenomenon watcher
attempting definition of undefinable,
wanting to fly into the vacuum to be born on the other side of space,
but keeping vigil on the cusp of realities and dreams.

I whisper a nebula from my ancient tongue,
a sigh of star dust from an inner cave that holds my Soul,
a vibration that only the Light in me understands,
only the OM that makes up my bones
realizes as saving grace,
and the pull of the black hole releases me.
I am no longer proton, neutron, electron,
I am beyond light and matter,
just Golden Transcending,
just independent radiant flight,
a shooting star,
a fiery comet,
a new-born galaxy whirling
trailblazer night-writer of light in the sky.
I become my own universe,
an everlasting song in the cosmos,
a vibration that ripples infinitely, infinity.

Inside us all,
there is a charge that is beyond positive and negative,
there is a frequency that ignites Divine,
there is the AUM that built your bones,
there is a blast of a brilliant supernova
that sparks from the calm of a pure Heart
linked with the Heart of the Sun,
and when you are

standing on the edge of a

BLACK HOLE

and every bit of light in you drains
into abysmal f o r g e t t i n g,

Call on your Inner Fire.
Call on the intonations of your own Soul.
Remember your own Brilliance and Beauty.
Remember Who You Are.

We are born of moments and lifetimes,
reciprocated energies,
recapitulated spirals of learning and detaching,
momentary relapses of pain and new life hatching.
We are Spiritual Beings in human bodies.
We are Celestial Bodies in limited skies,
but we must never fail to realize there is a purpose to all of this;

There is a New World on the Horizon,
and we are building it.

## ⌘ Star Birth M82

Go outside in this,
brave the freeze breeze
and beg for cloudless patch of open sky,
plead with streetlights
to dumb down their humming,
their white-blotting out of night,
their brightening blinding false light
that blocks you
from swallowing space into your chest,
prohibits dreaming,
white noise meditation,
step out there and look beyond the city,
find a space of silence
to witness the explosion birth
of a previously unseen star,
a supernova delivering a sun,
its magnitude and luminosity
reaching our peering earth's view
from 12 million light years away,
reflecting all wavelengths of visible light,
full spectrum of color,
glowing golden white.

Go outside for this,
bring your lover,
your mother,
your dog,
your friend or brother,
or bring your own inner peace and wanting,
and one day,

you can say, you saw a STAR being born,
tell your grandchildren,
call your father,
write a poem,
hold it in,
put it in a box marked forever,
unblot the night of glowing windows,
periscope yourself out of tattered skylines,
and sit in the ladle of big dipper mouth,
swing your legs back and forth,
incite gravitational shifting,
monkey bar stars,
make unbroken circles out of your hands
and binocular your eyes,
go be a part of this cosmic surprise
12 million years in the making,
let your insides... sunrise.

This star has burned for 12 million years,
yet to us, looking up into night,
it was born yesterday,
contorting our sense of time seeing something that is "now,"
but always "has been,"
but "always," too, is relative
to beginnings and ends,
and who is asking, and who is counting.
This star birth warps linear conclusions,
bends them backward like bridges,
over and under dimensions,
crossing the multiverse of infinity,
forming a string of invisible pearls
in the ether of all our yesterdays and tomorrows.

Perhaps, this star is the light of your own soul,
dawning flare on a far off horizon,
daybreaking your stubborn, worried heart.

Perhaps, it is the promise the Soul of our planet made
to this physical dirt and hurt earth,
that, yes, there will be a way to get out of all of this.

Perhaps our big bang galaxy birth is still reaching out,
forever casting light into the unfathomable distances of space,
and tonight the starlings of M82 can finally see us in their night sky.

Perhaps, it is just a moment
to be a part of incomprehensible magic,
the bending of time,
the ocean of rushing light waves
reaching the weary shores of our eyes,
however you want to see it,
just SEE it,
go outside.

## ⌘ Ashes

Ashes.
Cover me in ashes,
not just the little cross on my forehead,
lift up the soot and cinder of
something beautiful burned and bathe me
in a veil of blackness,
cover me so that I glint with the luster
of beaten coal held against the unforgiving sun,
knowing that this is my contrition.

Yes, I have forgotten God,
I left him on the side of the road
on my way to enlightenment.
I am going back but going forward.
I am turning my cheek to an abrasive wind
that sings of my empty songs,
that whispers the echoes of everything I scream
in my fits of darkness,
in my raging against the light,
in my taking of hostages,
in every ruthless battle I try to fight
against the Beautiful Self being born in me.

What can I burn that hasn't already caught fire
by the singe of my tongue
against a sleepless night?
I am not 100% light,
but I can see a broken mirror falling away,
the broken image prison can become a prism if I first
cover myself in ashes,

blackened face, body, hands, feet,
my defiance and ego painting me in the remains of fire,
make my body a prayer,
take my hands and form a steeple
that points only in the direction of the eastern star.

I am a striving spirit,
covered in the ashes of a burning earth,
covered in the sins that create this blissless mortality.
It took walking my path to realize the importance of ashes and dust,
this sacramental preparation of acknowledging
my own shadows before letting all the Light in,
of preparing a temple to hold my own Fiery Heart,
of knowing that God is the path and God is the traveler,
and that the atoms of coal will rearrange themselves,
under high heat and high pressure,
to become the atoms of diamonds.

I have walked into the fire willingly,
become the body covered in ash
so that I can be born a brilliant diamond.

Shoot me, incessantly, with a beam of light
until I bend it into a rainbow.

## ⌘ Valentine for a Vacant Womb

This is a Valentine
for what is unborn
in the space
below my belly button.
There is an empty room there,

(( my vacant womb ))

waiting for divine intervention,
miracles and angels on clouds,
a quiet-filled wanting,
unspoken hoping,
baby, someday maybe,
wish you were now.

I put up curtains
but I won't say what color.
I am building a crib from my ribcage,
and I know that the perfect temperature of milk
will be the warmth that comes out of my breasts.

Baby.
I love you.
Oh god, I love you.
I want to feel you growing into life,
I want to hear your heartbeat rhythm syncopation,
muffled and glowing with mine,
I want to sing to you, silly and sweet,
I want to make up words that you could grow into,
I want to write poems about your smile,

and the light in your eyes,
and how your cry sounds like it might be Heaven,
little one, my little one,
I have cupped my arms into cradle,
and rocked the weight of my spare tire belly to sleep,
and it almost feels like life and giving up, combined.
I did it more than once
even though it made me feel small,
just to practice the moves of mommy,
if you ever come.

This is a Valentine
for how your tiny toes crinkle
when I kiss them for the millionth time,
and how your tiny hand around my finger
makes me feel like I finally belong in this world,
and how you look at me and never look away,
and how you smell like spring rain at any time of day,
and how the sounds you make when dreaming
are enough for me to call music, forever.

Little darling,
I am waiting for you,
here is my open heart,
and my cradle hands,
and somewhere in the stars,
you are wondering where your home will be,
and I am here making myself into a home,
adding windows to my chest,
open-dooring my mouth
so that everything I say is beauty,
and life, and wonder.

I am readying a temple inside

(( my vacant womb ))

lighting a single candle,
turning poems into lullabies,
painting the ceiling with clouds,
shifting weight on my hips
back and forth
like a constant ocean,
thinking of what name I will call you
that means:

EVERYTHING.

# ⌘ Love, as Told by Poets

*A Cento\**

While the rose said to the sun, "I shall remember thee,"
her petals fell to the dust.
Under the night rug, the star rug, moon as lantern,
man in the moon watching over us, dog star at his heels, we lay.
As I predicted, now that I'm lying here next to her,
I feel only tenderness for the young woman by my side.

When you love, you should not say,
"God is in my heart," but rather, "I am in the heart of God."
And if the wine you drink, the Lip you press,
End in what All begins and ends in - Yes,
look, another window to see through,
like a woman was a drum, like a body was a weapon.
I step over her body while the black sun rises behind me,
smoking like an old pistol.

My love is an experience of absorption into all, all that exists.
At dawn, I walked along with a monk on his way to the monastery.
"We do the same work," I told him. "We suffer the same."
He gave me a bowl.
And I saw:
      the soul has *this* shape.
Fill our gold cups with love stirred into clear nectar.

I shudder sometimes to think of all that stellar mystery of how she
IS going to get me in a future lifetime, wow — And I seriously do
believe that will be my salvation, too.

The weight of the world, is love.

(Sources: Rabindranath Tagore, Jeanette Winterson, Paulo Coelho, Kahlil Gibran, Ani Difranco, Ai, Torkom Saraydarian, Rumi, Sappho, Jack Kerouac, Allen Ginsberg)

*From the Latin word for "patchwork," the cento (or collage poem) is a poetic form made up of lines from poems by other poets. Though poets often borrow lines from other writers and mix them in with their own, a true cento is composed entirely of lines from other sources.

## ⌘ For Maya, on this,
the Morning of Your Death

*"The caged bird sings*
*with a fearful trill*
*of things unknown*
*but longed for still*
*and his tune is heard*
*on the distant hill*
*for the caged bird*
*sings of freedom."*

You wrote a cage, a bird, the wind
into a song that has outlasted you,
as of this morning,
when North Carolina woke
missing the voice of a familiar breathing,
the bellowing rise and fall chest of treasures
sleeping through your last night into the
early morn, and the dawn of this day
rising on your noble face for the last time.

How many lives did you turn into
moments of gold with your open heart,
and your wise words, permeating the veil of history
with your unshakable truth and muted mouth
reborn into glory, little girl,
tell me a story
of how you did not talk for years,
how you thought it was your voice that killed that man
who took your eight year old body as his own,
how he spent one night in jail,
how your uncles took the law into their own just hands,

116

and no, child, your voice did not kill him,
yet five years went by without a word from your lips
because you thought your voice would kill anyone,
muted Marguerite, when your mouth finally opened again,
and when the pen was put there years later,
it was your voice that saved so many like you,
like myself, like all of us who turned to your words
as candles and as beacons and as hope.

Tell me a story of a young woman,
a young mother, driven to survival and necessity,
how sex and struggle became synonymous with life,
how poverty and prostitution
left a bitter pill in your mouth that you learned
to chew up into the words of songs,
night clubs knew your name, dark girl flame,
how you danced and sang Miss Calypso tuned
lullabies to your baby boy growing fight,
young and fast Marguerite Ann Johnson,
becoming Maya, becoming Maya Angelou,
girl you, YOU, were leaving your marks on the night,
and all of these fingerprints would soon turn to light.

Tell me a story of those Great Men,
and how you were a force under their feet,
how you were a fire in their bellies,
how you surely kept them on their toes
and graced them with your woman song,
how Dr. King and Malcolm X knew you as Sister,
how you picked up their blown out torches
and carried them into darkest cities with your words to light them,
how Egypt and Africa and motherlands
are woven into the tapestry of your delicate skin,
Maya, you are the movement personified,

117

you carried the Light of justice, of peace, of equality,
and I know that tonight,
your brothers King, X, Baraka and many others
are celebrating a joyous homecoming.

Tell me a story of your words,
Maya Angelou,
My Angel, you,
poet and dreamer and teacher and light.
Your words are a legacy forever etched in us,
the flight of your caged bird heart gave us hope
that we would escape our own self-made prisons,
and through the steps of our own growing,
and the compassion we extend to our brokenness, we can FLY.

Tell me one last story, My Angel.
I wonder if you were scared. Were you?
I wonder if you knew you were going to go. Did you?
I wonder what nightgown you chose to wear,
how you left your hair, pushed back and white, untouched silk.
I wonder if you felt alone, beautiful Poet,
or if you closed your eyes
in the presence of everyone you ever loved,
defying time and space
and gravity and place
and hearing only the hum of their hearts.
I wonder if you went to sleep
with peace resting heavily on your chest,
a shimmer in your eyes,
a knowing smile on your lips,
that's how I see you going,
silently slipping out of this world,
leaving the indelible marks of a Queen
on everything you touched.

I think of your last public words:
"Listen to yourself and in that quietude
you might hear the voice of God."
I listen to myself, to my heart, to my stories, to your stories,
to the unbreakable voice of women,
yes, all women,
rising up in a song of sisterhood,
rising in a handholding pact of solidarity,
rising up in waves of love that light a path to your Transcendence.

In my heart, I fly with you this morning,
just for a moment, to feel the wind underneath your golden wings,
to see the rainbows that are rising out of clouds
that remind us of the color you left in the world
with your Beauty, your Message, your Spirit, your Freedom.

Rest In Poetry, Maya Angelou.

April 4, 1928 - May 28, 2014

## ⌘ Heirloom

Make my mouth an heirloom
that you can hide away,
that you can pass on,
pass down to your children,
locket tuck in gold around your tender neck,
hold it inside a mahogany hope chest
to save for merciless winters, or rainy days
or weddings or births or loneliness,
where you will want to remember
the way that I could make your body tingle at
the toss of a vowel, the thread of sound
that I string together to make nouns
that leave you breathless
and waiting,
on the edge,
on the line between desire and dreams,
on the precipice of listening and screaming
your love into the howl of a night,
knowing I would recognize your moon.

heirloom.

# ⌘ Willing My Body Parts

This is the last will and testament of all my body parts.

I leave my right forefinger, middle finger and thumb
joined into a clover of digits,
to every pen in the world
that will write everything that is beauty,
or that needs justice, or that needs a voice.

I leave my brain,
to the soil, plant it like a seed
where ideas that never came to fruition
can blossom into flowered manifestation,
be picked up by the winds like glowing spores,
and change the world for the better.

I leave my shoulder blades to
the other angels on earth who forgot who they are,
who forgot that
there are wings attached to their shoulder blades
that are invisible here,
that can only be seen in the other worlds,
that vibrate with the frequency of a million hummingbirds,
and that are yours.

I leave the swoop from under my nose
to my top lip, a favorite tiny finger slide, to my first love,
who always touched me there before she kissed me,
it's those little things that love leaves in
your memory, that sustain.

My lips?

I leave my lips to the poets,
for every word that I tried to speak
for every word that never came out quite right,
or loud enough, or to the right ears,
may you pick up my mouth like a torch,
and use it for the only purpose I had for it;
Light.

Speaking of fire,
I leave my volcano thighs
to the islands of Hawaii and Fiji
where they can again return as heated mounds of earth,
lava eager to explode
and form new words and worlds
that people can pray to,
and pray around,
and pray for.

And my breasts,
I leave my breasts to all the babies that
needed a mother, that never were held that close,
that never were rocked in the ocean of a mother's bosom.
Use my breasts as all of the mothers' milk,
as soft mountains,
as pillows,
as comfort, as love.

My neck,
I leave to every cause I stuck my neck out for;
equality,
gay rights,
bullying,
suicide,
drug addiction,

don't ask don't tell,
loving her,
loving her,
loving her,
talking to my high school students like they were people, not
robots.
Yes, my neck was out there for you,
and I would put it out there again.

My voice,
I leave to the quiet ones,
to the meek minuscule mice
that whisper their dreams to darkened rooms,
and wish only to be heard,
and wish only to have something to say worth hearing,
and wish they were the boisterous center
of every crowd, that laughs were because of their joy
and their gravity-defying smile,
voice, here.
Take it.
Hear.

My ears,
I leave my ears to the night sounds,
the chorus of frogs in the Arkansas moonlight,
the whip-poor-will that constantly searches and sings,
the harmony of crickets and silence and breathing,
and snoring of a little dog,
and silent sleep of loved ones close,
the night sounds always moved me still.

Still,
I moved in this life,
took steps alone sometimes,

in the dark,
away,
together again,
took steps to better my world,
took steps to create change,
took steps on narrow, size 7 and a half feet
that held the frame of an ever-fluctuating body,
I leave my feet to the footprints I made at the summit
of no imaginary mountain. Leave them there in the place
cut out of the earth for them,
in all of their glory,
a part of the sky.

My eyes,
I leave my eyes to the next thing
on this path that is defined as Beauty,
leave the pair fixed on that Beautiful thing,
whatever it may be; a sunset, a handful of roses,
a baby's feet, a kiss, a snow angel, anything, as
long as it is Beauty,
I leave them as a pinpoint on a map of home,
a compass,
a mile marker,
a magnet,
pulling me to the only thing that really matters.

Love.
My heart had so much love here,
so much that it burst open and became every atom,
every cell, every wondrous and magical thing.
I leave my heart to you...
You know who you are.
You showed me the moon from
the other side of our galaxy,

You named my body Beauty.
You took my heart and always held it
like a breakable fragile thing;
it's only fitting that you should keep it,
since it will be yours when I come back again,
this reoccurring dream that is our love.

As for the rest of my body parts,
don't bury them,
don't make me any more of this earth than I already had to be,
the gravity weighs heavy and I am not made for worms.

Set me on fire and let me rise to the Sun.

Leave all of me to the Sun.

# About the Author

Author photography by Ester Coggin

Kai Coggin is a full-time poet and freelance writer born in Bangkok, Thailand, raised in Southwest Houston, and currently a blip in the 3-million acre Ouachita National Forest in Hot Springs, AR. She holds a Bachelor of Arts in Poetry and Creative Writing from Texas A&M University. She writes poems of feminism, love, spirituality, injustice, metaphysics, and beauty. Kai has been published in *Elephant Journal*, *Cliterature*, *The Manila Envelope*, *[empath]*, *Catching Calliope* and an anthology to be released summer 2014 called *Journey of the Heart*. She released her first chapbook, *In Other Words*, in August 2013. PERISCOPE HEART is her first full-length collection of poetry.

Kai knows that words hold the potential to create monumental and global change, and she uses her words like a sword of Beauty. She can be found most Wednesdays at a local venue, reading her poems into an open mic, hoping the wind carries her words out to the world.

If you would like to contact Kai to arrange a poetry reading or book signing, please e-mail her at periscopeheart@gmail.com.